8.24

GUI

C

Kids Outdoor Gardening

Other books by Aileen Paul

Kids cooking (with Arthur Hawkins)
Kids Gardening: A First Indoor Garden-
    ing Book
Kids Camping
Candies, Cookies, Cakes (with Arthur
    Hawkins)
Kids Cooking Complete Meals
Kids Cooking Without a Stove
The Kids' 50-State Cookbook

Kids Outdoor Gardening

by **Aileen Paul**

illustrated by **John DeLulio**

Doubleday & Company, Inc.
GARDEN CITY, NEW YORK

Library of Congress Catalog Card Number 77–80902
ISBN 0-385-12757-x Trade
    0-385-12758-8 Prebound

contents

a word to kids

Would you like a garden? You don't have to be a magician to grow vegetables and flowers. The rules are simple and the work is fun.

You dig and plant and pull weeds, all at the right time, of course. And one fine day you proudly pick a bouquet of flowers or gather a basket of vine-ripe tomatoes or green beans.

You do, of course, need the right place to plant your garden. No magic wand can make a gardening site appear in front of you and your rake. If you live in a house, you can probably find an area in your yard.

If you live in an apartment, ask your teacher or club leader to help you and others develop a gardening project. A small parcel of land belonging to a nearby church, school, park, or industrial area might be available to a group. Many communities are sharing land for gardening these days.

You can also grow a number of vegetables (tomatoes and green peppers, for example) in containers on sunny window sills and terraces (Chapter 11).

You can receive help from local or county garden clubs as well as the Extension Service Agricultural Agent (listed in the phone book under the name of your county).

a word to adults

This book is planned as a simple beginning guide for children with suggestions for additional reading if needed.

For children, the joys of gardening are almost unlimited. Growing garden-fresh vegetables or fragrant flowers is a glorious activity in a world of packaged and synthetic products.

Taking part in the age-old practices of planting and harvesting can give youngsters a satisfactory feeling of self-fulfillment in a society where much activity may appear meaningless to them.

Children also reach an awareness of the importance of ecology when they work in the earth. They learn to care for and understand our vulnerable planet.

What is the role of adults in a child's gardening project? I think it will vary depending upon age and relationship. Most youngsters will need help in getting tools and supplies and advice on financing the project. Some physical assistance in getting the plot ready might be accepted.

You will definitely need to supervise carefully, or even *carry out,* any use of pesticides.

Perhaps a sympathetic attitude and cautious overseeing are the most important contributions you can offer, even though you may be tempted to participate.

Kids Outdoor Gardening

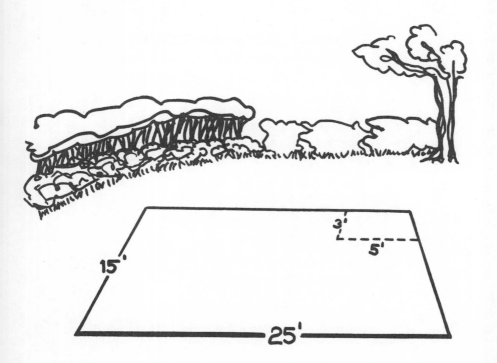

how you start

The size of your garden is the first thing to decide upon. That decision will depend on how much workable ground is available and on how much time you have.

You can have a successful garden in a small space, say 3 by 5 feet. A popular size today is 15 by 25 feet. You can also plant vegetables or flowers next to other plantings or shrubbery, but only if no dangerous pesticide has been used in that area over the past five years. That's important to remember.

13

For example, in addition to our small garden (10 by 12 feet) we grow lettuce and curly cress along the edge of the rock garden, tomatoes and peas in a 3-foot space by the driveway, and cucumbers running up the wooden fence.

Walk around outside to look over the space available. Your best guide to fertile ground is to choose an area where other plants have grown (grass, flowers, or weeds). You can expect to have success with a garden planted in such an area if you follow the suggestions in this book.

Here are specific things to look for in choosing a garden site:

1. Plenty of sunshine, 5 to 6 hours each day.
2. Almost level ground so that rain will not wash away seeds and plants. A gentle slope, however, helps drainage.
3. A nearby faucet for watering.
4. Soil that is fairly free of rocks.

14

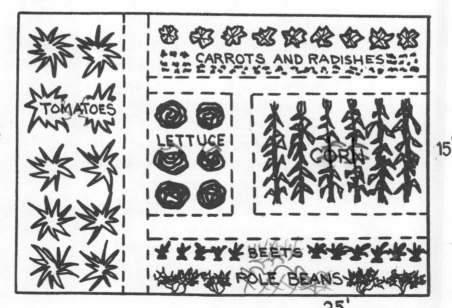

15'

25'

If an area seems suitable, you might make arrangements for a soil test through the Extension Service Agricultural Agent (Chapter 13). Do-it-yourself Soil Testing kits are available from many seed companies. The results would tell you what the soil needs to be most productive. You can still do a proper job of preparing the garden site without a soil test, however.

When you have found the right place for your garden, and received permission to use it, try to figure out how much time you can spend gardening. Will you be working alone, with a friend, or with someone in your family? Is it to be a class or club project? It is important to plant only as much as you can comfortably take care of.

POSSIBLE ROW ARRANGEMENT
FOR A GARDEN 15 X 25 FEET*

(with names of plants that can be added later)

Feet

Feet	
00	Tomatoes, staked. Interplant with lettuce plants.
3	Snap beans.
5½	Early carrots. Follow with fall cabbage plants.
8	Pepper plants.
11	Eggplant. Interplant with lettuce.
13½	Early beets. Follow with 4 hills of vine squash.
16	Early bush peas. Follow with late snap beans.
18½	6 hills of summer squash. Follow with fall carrots, turnips.
21	Cucumbers up fence or trellis.
25	

Follow directions on seed packets or in seed catalogues.

*Adapted from "Plan Your Vegetable Garden," Leaflet #329, U. S. Department of Agriculture.

Now you are ready to plan your garden on paper. The chart on the facing page may be helpful. Use it only as a guide for your own choices. If you need help on the right plants, write or call the County Agricultural Agent and ask for "Home Garden Vegetable Variety Recommendations" for your state.

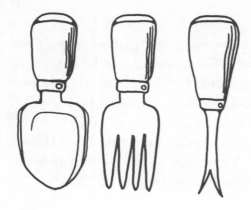

chapter 2

tools and other things

To plant a garden, you need certain tools and other things to work with.

If your family owns gardening tools, ask permission to borrow them. If they do not, perhaps you can borrow from a friendly neighbor or relative. In either case, promise to take care of them and return them promptly.

If you need to buy tools, watch for sales at hardware stores or "garage" sales. You do not have to spend a large amount of money although you should buy well-made tools.

The right tools make work easier, of course, although it is possible to garden

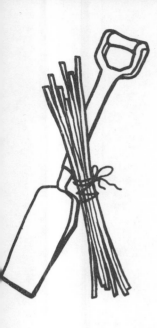

with a few essential pieces. One year my children and I planted a small garden with the fewest tools possible.

here's what we used:

a spade (or shovel) to turn the ground

a metal rake to smooth the ground

a long-handled hoe to dig trenches for planting

a watering can or hose

metal or wooden stakes for large plants (sturdy branches will do)

a trowel

sturdy twigs or short branches for small plants

markers (ice cream sticks saved throughout the year)

string to mark the rows

inexpensive gardening gloves

The following hand tools are helpful but not essential:

a cultivator
a weeder

Tools must be taken care of properly. Return them after use to a protected place—garage, basement, or shed. Brush the dirt off first with an old rag. Wipe the metal part with a clean rag dipped lightly in oil every two or three weeks to prevent rust.

20 fertilizers

You will find it easier to use commercial fertilizers to feed your growing plants rather than manure, even if it is available.

Commercial fertilizers carry a number, like 5–10–5, or 5–10–10. To be very simple, the first number is the nitrogen; the second is the phosphate; and the third is the potassium; all needed for healthy growth.

The ones I have suggested in this book are for general use. As you become more experienced, you may want to use special fertilizers for certain plants. All fertilizers are carefully labeled and carry a world of information on the package.

a compost pile

As a beginning gardener, you should learn what compost is. It is a mixture of dead leaves, flowers, vegetable tops and peelings, leaves, grass clippings, and other organic material with fertilizer added. This organic material decays and you then return it to the garden to make the soil more workable and fertile.

Because your time and space are probably limited, it seems to me that a compost pile should wait until you are older. A compost must be prepared carefully and begun in the summer for the following spring. Once started, you must continue watering and adding layers of material.

You can, however, compost in a less ambitious fashion by using shredded leaves, grass clippings, or hay to cover the ground between rows and around plants.

If you have space for wide rows (so that there is no danger of hurting the roots of established plants), you can make a "mini compost pile" by digging narrow deep holes in the rows. Fill the holes with carrots and radish tops, or other organic material. Sprinkle with a small amount of fertilizer and cover with the soil taken from the hole. The organic material will rot quickly and provide food for your growing plants.

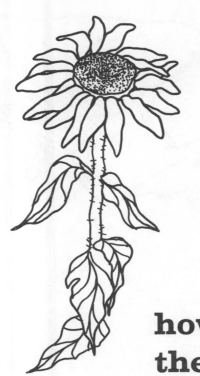

chapter 3

how to prepare the ground

When the first mild days arrive in the spring, gardeners are eager to begin. Work outside must wait, however, until the ground has begun to warm up and dry out from seasonal rains.

Keep in mind as you read this chapter that the exact type of soil is not as important as some of the factors mentioned earlier. It is helpful to have the soil test made (Chapter 1), but the ground can be made fertile and workable without the test.

For a successful garden, you need deep, well-drained, and preferably crumbly soil. Crush a clod of dirt between your

23

fingers and you will learn something of its texture.

> Silt feels crumbly and breaks up between your fingers.
> Clay soil seems glued together. It will need extra peat moss.
> Sandy soil slides through your fingers. It will need extra top soil and peat moss.

Here are the steps to be taken to ready the ground for planting:

1. Mark area to be planted with 4 short stakes, one at each corner. Tie a long piece of string from stake to stake to show boundaries.
2. Clear the area of plant growth.
3. Spread about 2 inches of organic material (peat moss or shredded leaves) over the ground.
4. Spread ground limestone at the rate of 10 pounds per 100 square feet, or 5

pounds per 50 square feet. (Limestone is added the first time you prepare a new garden site but not after
that unless tests show it is needed.)

5. Spread a 5–10–5 or 5–10–10 fertilizer
   at the same rate as limestone. (See
   fertilizers in previous chapter.)
6. Work these materials into the soil by
   using the spade or shovel. Spade to a
   depth of about 6 inches by pushing
   the spade straight down with your
   foot. Pull the handle back. Turn
   spade to right, loosening the soil.
   Move on to the left and repeat the
   action.
   (If you have a large space, try to
   make arrangements for a rotary tiller
   which turns the earth. See note at end
   of chapter.)
7. Break up clods of dirt with bottom of
   metal rake.
8. Rake ground evenly. Remove any
   rocks or sticks.

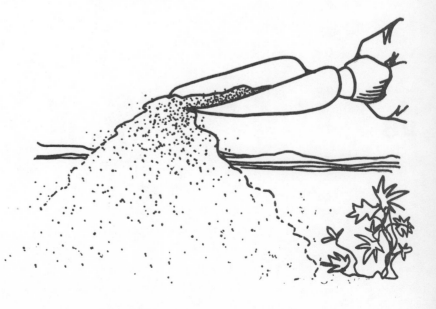

Be of good cheer; the work does not have to be done in one day. Your labor can be spread out over several days. The results of your effort will be properly prepared crumbly soil.

Worms, the gardener's friends, can then tunnel around, loosening the ground and speeding decay of organic material. The roots of plants will find it easier to make their way downward, and water can circulate freely.

> NOTE: The rotary garden tiller should be used *by an adult*. It is helpful in preparing the soil for planting. Frequently rotary tillers can be rented from a garden center, or the service is available for renting by the hour.

chapter 4

what to plant

Plant the vegetables you like to eat and the flowers you like to see and smell. Choose those that grow well in your part of the country.

Information in the seed catalogues and on the seed packets will help you decide. You might ask for advice from a neighboring gardener, someone familiar with your soil and climate. By all means, write or call the County Agricultural Agent (Chapter 13), and ask questions of the garden center dealer from whom you buy.

To give you some idea of what you

27

might plant, among the easy-to-grow vegetables and flowers are:

Snap beans	Peas
Beets	Peppers
Carrots	Radishes
Cucumbers	Squash
Leaf lettuce	Tomatoes
Four O'Clocks	Petunias
Impatiens	Portulaca
Marigolds	Sunflowers
Nasturtiums	Zinnias

As you will read in the next chapter, the time of planting is important. Plants are grouped in a chart at the end of this chapter according to their hardiness, which means according to their temperature requirements. You need that information when selecting seeds or plants.

Among other things to consider in choosing vegetables and flowers are:

1. The number of days from planting until harvesting.
2. The amount of care needed.
3. Adaptability of the soil. (If the soil is packed and not loose enough, root vegetables such as beets and carrots may be unable to push their way down. Beans and cucumbers, on the other hand, might do well.)

Buy best quality disease-free flowers and vegetable seeds and plants. In many cases you may prefer to buy plants, such

as green pepper, tomato, or eggplant, instead of seeds to give you an earlier growing season.

As I mentioned before, the information contained in the seed catalogues is useful. That's why gardeners look forward to their arrival during the winter to help in planning. For example, here's a description of Green Bush Snap Beans:

how to grow bush snap beans:

Plant seeds when danger of frost is past and the soil is warm. Make furrows (trenches) 2 inches deep and space the beans 2 to 3 inches apart.

Mature in 50 days . . . real vigor, adaptability, and resistance to adverse weather.

You can see that it is important to know what to plant and when.

when to plant

The urge to plant, as we said earlier, often comes with the first sunny and warm days. Keep in mind, however, that the earth must change from winter chill and damp to warmth in which seeds can sprout.

How are we to know when the time for planting arrives? Our ancestors planted by following the natural schedule of wild plants. I remember that my grandmother always told me, "Plant when the oak leaves are the size of a squirrel's ears." That is a sign, of course, that the ground is warming up and the trees are beginning to leaf out.

Although many modern gardeners say that they seed when familiar trees and shrubs are in leaf or bloom, they are obviously following the sensible rule of planting after danger of frost is past. The frost date can be gotten from local gardeners, from newspaper gardening columns, or from the County Agricultural Agent (Chapter 13).

Another guide to keep in mind is that vegetables should be planted according to how much cold or hot weather they can stand. To be specific, here is a timetable for some of the popular vegetables. The spring frost-free date is 2 to 3 weeks after the average date of the last freeze.

Some common vegetables grouped according to the approximate times they can be planted and their relative requirements for cool and warm weather.

Cold-hardy plants for early-spring planting		Cold-tender or heat-hardy plants for later-spring or early-summer planting			Hardy plants for late-summer or fall planting except in the North
Very hardy	Hardy	Not cold-hardy (Tender)	Requiring hot weather	Medium heat-tolerant	
Broccoli	Beet	Bean,	Bean,	Bean,	Beet
Cabbage	Carrot	snap	lima	all	Collard
Lettuce	Chard	Okra	Eggplant	Chard	Kale
Onion	Mustard	New Zea-	Pepper	Soybean	Lettuce
Pea	Parsnip	land	Sweet	New Zea-	Mustard
Potato	Radish	spinach	potato	land	Spinach
Spinach		Soybean	Cucumber	spinach	Turnip
Turnip		Squash	Melon	Squash	
		Sweet		Sweet	
		corn		corn	
		Tomato			

Table 3. "Growing Vegetables in the Home Garden," Home and Garden Bulletin #202, U. S. Department of Agriculture.

31

You know, of course, that the earlier you successfully plant, the earlier you will have vegetables and flowers to enjoy. Early, midseason, and late planting will also help make the most of your garden.

succession planting

This important-sounding expression, *succession planting*, means to follow one crop with another in the same season. For example, early peas may be followed by carrots or beets, beans by cabbage, etc.

Always work fertilizer into the soil before replanting.

planting by the moon cycle

32

Lively discussions take place among gardeners, young and old, about planting when the moon is new or full. Everyone is quite sure that their way is right.

As you know, the moon and sun affect the tides and there is a gravitational pull on the earth. There is no scientific proof, however, of its effect on gardening. My father and grandparents, successful gardeners, considered planting by the light of the moon seriously. If you want to experiment, The Old Farmer's Almanac has a Planting and Garden Calendar.

The general rule is to plant "above-ground" vegetables (peas, lettuce, etc.) from the new moon until the full moon. Plant root vegetables (carrots, beets, etc.) when the moon is waning.

33

VEGETABLE GUIDE

NAME AND TYPE	HARDI-NESS-	DAYS TO GERMINATE	DAYS TO HARVEST	HOW FAR APART	SUGGESTIONS
Beans, snap, bush, and pole	Tender	7–14	50–60	18–30 inches	Plant every 2 weeks until midsummer. Pole beans need sturdy poles. Bush beans are helped by stakes.
Beets, red, golden, white	Hardy	10–21	55–80	18–24 inches	Plant every 2 weeks until early summer.
Carrots	Hardy	7–14	65–75	12 inches	Choose variety best for soil; short root types for shallow or heavy soil. Plant again in midsummer for fall harvest.
Cress, garden or water	Hardy	3–14	10–50	6–12 inches	Plant garden or curly cress every 2 weeks. Grow watercress in moist shade.
Cucumbers	Tender	7–14	53–65	4–5 feet	Grow on fence to save space. Keep picking to encourage new fruit.
Lettuce, leaf	Hardy	7–14	40–47	14 inches	Plant in spring and another late summer.
Lettuce, head	Hardy	7–14	65–90	14 inches	Needs cool weather in spring or fall to make a good head.
Peas, dwarf	Hardy	7–14	55–79	Double rows, 3 inches apart	Plant as early as ground can be worked.

NAME AND TYPE	HARDI-NESS-	DAYS TO GERMINATE	DAYS TO HARVEST	HOW FAR APART	SUGGESTIONS
Peppers	Tender	10–21	60–77	18 inches	Best to buy plants.
Pumpkins	Tender	7–14	95–120	Plant in "hills" 6–8 feet apart	
Radishes	Hardy	7–14	22–60	1–2 inches	Make plantings every few weeks until early summer; again in fall.
Tomatoes	Tender	7–14	52–86	If staked, 18 inches apart in rows 3–4 feet	Best to buy plants, include early bearing and midseason.
Squash, summer	Tender	7–14	48–60	Plant in "hills" 3–4 feet apart	Keep fruits picked so plants produce more.

FLOWER GUIDE

NAME	HARDINESS	DAYS TO GERMINATE	GROWING SUGGESTIONS
Candytuft	Hardy	14–21	Sun. Takes heat, drought, poor or sandy soil.
Coleus	Tender	7–21	Sun to partial shade outdoors. Sunny windowsill or under Gro-Lux lights indoors.
Four O'Clock	Tender	10–14	Sun. Takes heat, drought, poor or sandy soil.
Impatiens	Tender	10–21	Blooms well in shade, especially in hot summer areas.
Marigold	Tender	7–14	Sun. Takes heat, drought, poor or sandy soil.
Nasturtium	Half-hardy	7–14	Sun. Takes heat, drought, poor or sandy soil.
Petunia	Half-hardy	7–21	Sun. Takes heat, drought, poor or sandy soil.
Phlox	Half-hardy	14–21	Sun. Takes heat, drought, poor or sandy soil.
Portulaca	Tender	7–14	Sun. Takes heat, drought, poor or sandy soil.
Stock	Hardy	10–21	Sun to partial shade.
Strawflower	Tender	7–14	Sun. Pick flowers for drying just as they open, remove from foliage, bunch loosely, and hang heads downward in a cool, airy place.
Sunflower	Tender	7–14	Sun. Takes heat, drought, poor or sandy soil.
Zinnia	Tender	7–14	Sun. Takes heat, drought, poor or sandy soil, but blooms best when well watered.

Vegetable and Flower Guide adapted from "Gardening for Pleasure," W. Atlee Burpee Company.

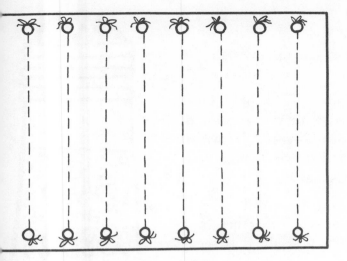

chapter 6

how to plant

Follow the chart you made on paper. Begin in the garden by placing stakes at the end of the first row. Now measure the space between each row and place stakes. Mark rows with a string tied between the stakes. Continue until you have completed marking the entire garden, or you can mark the rows that are first to be planted.

Dig the rows you intend to plant first; peas, for example. Make a shallow trench directly under the string using a hoe or rake handle. Make it only as deep as the seed packet tells you; half inch, one inch, whatever; too deep and

37

the plants cannot come up through the ground.

Planting larger seeds (beans, peas, etc.) goes quickly because they are easy to handle. Planting smaller seeds (radishes, lettuce, carrots, and others) takes patience because of their size.

Some gardeners find it useful to mix small seeds and fine sand together in a large salt shaker before seeding. If seeds are bunched in the ground, they grow that way, of course; and it is difficult to thin them later. Sometimes the seeds cannot even sprout because they are stacked upon each other.

After the seeds are in the ground, cover with garden soil or top soil. Pat soil firmly but lightly.

Mark the stakes with name of plant and planting date. Keep your original chart and seed packets for reference.

Seed tape planting is relatively new. By this method the seeds are evenly spaced on organic, water soluble tapes. The tapes are particularly useful for the tiny seeds I mentioned.

setting out plants

Plants that you buy from the nursery (or grow yourself) are best transplanted in the late afternoon to avoid the heat. About an hour before transplanting, water containers carefully and drain. Some gardeners, if the ground is dry, water each hole ½ hour before transplanting, making certain not to over-water.

Prepare holes for all plants before you begin resetting to avoid harmful drying out. Space according to chart in Chapter 5, or recommended distances suggested by the garden center.

Dig each hole wider and deeper than the plant and its clinging soil. Remove small rocks and sticks from hole. Refill with some amount of soil so that the plant will be at ground level with roots covered when set into earth. With a trowel, knife, or your hands, separate the first plant from the others. Keep as much soil with roots as possible. Reset the plant at the same depth at which it was growing. Press soil around roots firmly with your hands.

39

Continue until all plants are reset. Water enough to moisten the ground but not saturate it. Place stakes or supports in before you transplant large plants like eggplant and tomato.

chapter 7

taking care of your garden

general care

Keep your garden weed-free. Weeds take nourishment from the soil around your plants. If your garden is small, pull weeds by hand as soon as they appear. If your garden is large, remove them with a hoe.

40 "Which are weeds?" is a question frequently asked by first-time gardeners. Look carefully at the seedlings growing in the rows you have planted, then look at the newcomers growing between the rows, and you will be able to tell which are weeds.

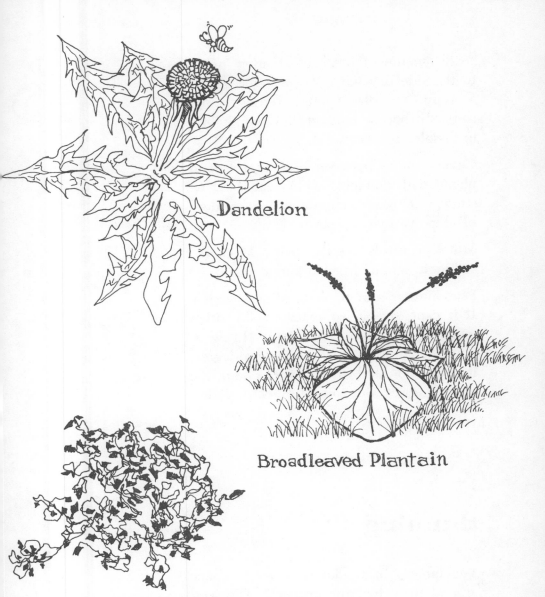

Dandelion

Broadleaved Plantain

Common chickweed

Here are three common garden weeds: Narrowleaf and Broadleaved Plantain, Dandelion, and Chickweed.

When plants are 3 or 4 inches high, it is time to fertilize (Chapter 2). Sprinkle a small amount of fertilizer about 3 inches to the side of each row (a coffee can is a useful utensil). Scratch fertilizer into soil with hoe or cultivator. Water lightly to dissolve fertilizer.

Cover ground between rows and around plants with "mulch," which can be hay, straw, or grass clippings, or modern black polyethylene (plastic film).

Mulch controls weeds, helps keep the soil moist and at an even temperature.

Peat moss is sometimes used as a mulch. It is expensive in comparison with other mulches, although convenient. However, while it controls weeds to some degree, it tends to hold the moisture and the ground dries out more quickly underneath.

thinning

Vegetables and flowers need space around them to grow properly. The seed packet gives exact information on how much space. When gardeners "thin," they pull out the extra plants.

Thinning should be done when seedlings are 2 or 3 inches tall. Carefully pull out the extra seedlings when the soil is

2-3" TALL

damp. Try not to disturb the remaining plants. Usually seedlings are thrown away (or buried), but some plants, like lettuce or spinach, can be transplanted.

keeping tidy

Do not allow trash, old leaves, and sticks to pile up. They make a breeding place for insects.

If there are several sick-looking plants, pull them up immediately. Get rid of them right away. Wash your hands and any tools to avoid spreading the disease.

watering

Nature's rainfalls are best, of course, but often fail us. In that case, water thoroughly once a week so that moisture

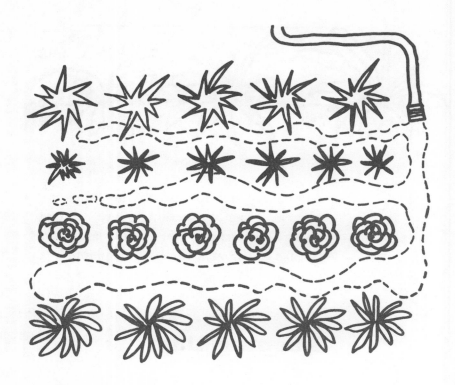

goes down about 4 inches for plants and 1 inch for seedlings.

The best way to water is to run the water between the rows for the entire length until soil is soaked. You can also use a sprinkler or spray nozzle of the hose.

Water slowly so that no puddles are formed. You will begin to understand why gardeners speak lovingly of soft rains.

staking

For an efficient small garden with average soil, plants that grow over 1½ feet high should be staked.

Pole beans need sturdy 5- or 6-foot poles dug at least 1½ feet into the ground. Bush beans need a 3- to 4-foot stake.

Eggplant and pepper plants need a strong support like a 4-foot stake dug well into the ground.

Peas can be supported by actual brush taken from hedges or trees. You can buy netting to use in place of brush.

Tomato plants can be kept upright with stout stakes, 6 or 7 feet long and driven 2 feet into the ground. A new and inexpensive heavy mesh can be bought at garden centers or hardware stores.

There are lively discussions about the way in which you tie plants to stakes. Some gardeners favor strips of cotton from old sheets or shirts; others use plastic plant ties. You need a strong tie but one that does not cut into the plant. Use whatever is easiest, cheapest, and works best for you.

You may need some help from an older person when you drive in the stakes.

45

insect and
disease control

Two classes of bugs and insects generally attack plants in the garden. The first are sucking insects like aphids, red spiders, and mealy bugs. The second are chewing insects like beetles, certain worms, and grubs.

There are strong arguments among gardeners about handling insects and diseases. We will try to cover both points of view, without chemicals and with them.

You will know when a plant needs help by the way it looks. The leaves may be

46

chewed, turned yellow, or wilted. That usually means pests have been at work.

"companion planting" as prevention

Many gardeners feel that "companion planting" (planting certain combinations of plants together) will keep insects away. Some scientific research has been done, primarily on marigolds. You may enjoy carrying out your own research. My vegetable garden is scattered with surprising little plants. Here are some that I have experimented with:

1. Marigolds to give off a substance that kills parasitic worms called "nematodes."
2. Chives and garlic are said to keep insects away.
3. Mint is supposed to keep ants and cabbage-worm butterflies at a distance.
4. Nasturtiums make squash bugs unhappy, some people say.
5. The striped cucumber beetle may not like radishes.

47

control without insecticides

Some insects can be controlled to some degree without insecticides. You can get help from lady bugs, praying mantises, birds, snakes, and toads because they eat insects. The first two can be ordered from seed companies and placed in your garden. Birds are encouraged to stay nearby with birdbaths and birdhouses.

here are other ways of coping with insects:

1. Aphids (very small soft-bodied insects in various colors and sizes): Spray with soap and water, 10 tablespoons of soap flakes to 3 gallons of water.
2. Japanese beetles (about ½ inch long and oval, shiny green with bronze wing covers and white hairs coming from under wing covers): Use small stick and knock them into large can partially filled with water. And there they drown.
3. Mexican beetles (light copper color and spotted): Knock off into can. You can also crush yellow egg masses with paper towel.
4. Mealy bugs (tiny soft bugs covered with cotton-like fluff): Clean off with cotton swabs soaked in alcohol or wash off with soap and water.

48

5. Cutworms (may be gray, brown, black, striped or spotted): A 3-inch cardboard collar placed around the stems of plants with 1 inch pressed down in the ground may stop them. A ring of wood ashes sometimes protects the plants.
6. Slugs (legless, slimy, soft-bodied creatures without shells. May be black, gray, or brown. They leave a slimy trail): Slugs are mostly night raiders. A border of sand, cinders, or wood ashes around the plant bed sometimes keeps them away. Their soft bodies are sensitive to those materials. An expensive control is to place shallow containers of beer around the plants. They drink and drown in the container.

insecticides and fungicides

It is difficult to garden without using chemical sprays, although organic gardeners are satisfied with their results. As I said earlier, cleanliness and best-quality plants will help.

If you do need additional help, read and

follow the instructions on the label of chemical sprays and powders carefully. Use them at the appropriate time; that's important.

The most frequently used insecticides contain rotenone or pyrethrum for vegetable plants. A Nicotine Solution is used on flowers. Make certain that flower sprays are kept away from vegetables. Sevin (a brand name for a chemical called carbaryl) is sometimes used for beans.

Captan is a safe control against fungus in the soil. *Here you need adult help.* And, once again, follow directions on the label.

chapter 9

harvesting

Harvesting is a joyful time as you gather vegetables and flowers. You can understand why great poems are written and paintings done about harvesting.

flowers

Pick your flowers when they are in full bloom. It encourages the plants to produce more flowers. Remove any faded blossoms and developing seed pods.

You might want to consider drying flowers such as strawflowers. I am sure your library has some excellent books on the subject.

Some flowers need extra attention: in midsummer cut off the tops of straggly alyssum plants and they will bloom again. Cut back snapdragons, salvia, and delphinium. They too will be encouraged to flower again later.

vegetables

How can you tell when vegetables are ready to harvest?

Snap beans should be picked as soon as you can barely see or feel the outline of the seeds underneath the pod cover.

Cabbage and head lettuce should be picked when the heads are formed and feel solid.

Leaf lettuce can be picked, leaf by leaf if you like, when it is about 3 inches high.

Tomatoes, of course, for the home gardener are picked vine ripe when the color is a lush red, or golden or-

ange if the variety is the orange one.

Summer squash should be picked when young while skin is tender. Some varieties can be left on the vine longer. Check the seed packet.

Beets and carrots are usually ready when the top is about 12 inches high. Pull one or two to see their size. These two root crops can stand a light frost.

You have a clue as to harvesting by the maturity date given in the chart, the average length of time from planting to maturity.

53

getting ready for next year

There are important steps to take in the fall which will help the soil become more fertile.

First, of course, the clean-up. Pull up vines and stems. Get rid of diseased ones. Bury the healthy ones in trenches throughout the garden site about 8 inches deep.

54 Look over the opening chapters to remind you of those things which help soil become productive. Following those suggestions, sprinkle lime lightly over the garden. By the spring it will have dissolved and added to the soil's nutrients.

Save fertilizing until the spring unless you want to add a slow-acting one like bone meal.

If you have wood or charcoal ashes available, apply them now over the garden site. They contain potash, an excellent soil conditioner.

Add a layer of shredded leaves, grass clippings, compost, or wood chips. In the northern part of our country, the ground is usually turned over with a spade. That exposes the earth to frost which kills some insects and helps decay organic matter. The ground is left rough. In the south, some gardeners do not turn the garden over.

planting in containers

If you do not have space outside for a garden, you can plant successfully in containers. They can be kept on a sunny windowsill, a balcony or terrace, or doorsteps.

Many of the suggestions in the earlier part of the book should be useful—planting, watering, and general care. Keep in mind that plant roots can go no deeper than the container. The plant, therefore, is dependent upon your care entirely. For more details you may want to read my book *Kids Gardening: A First Indoor Gardening Book for Children.* For this type of gardening you will need containers, soil, seeds or plants, and fertilizer.

containers

Use large clay or plastic pots, plastic or metal pails, or ready-made boxes of plastic, metal, or wood. The size and number depend on how many plants you want to grow.

If the containers do not have holes for drainage, put 1 or 2 inches of coarse gravel or rocks in the bottom of each container.

Large plastic plates or trays placed under the containers will keep water stains from forming on the wood under the container.

57

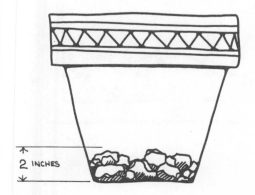

2 INCHES

soil

Ordinary garden soil usually contains too many organisms for container planting.

A soil substitute can be gotten from seed dealers and garden supply centers. It is free of plant disease, organisms, and weed seed, is lightweight, and holds moisture.

You can make your own soil substitute, but the cost will be about the same. Mix ½ bushel each of vermiculite and

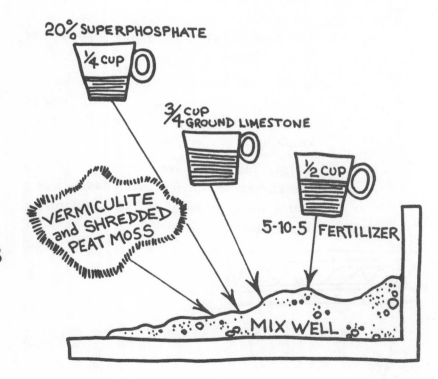

20% SUPERPHOSPHATE

¼ CUP

¾ CUP GROUND LIMESTONE

½ CUP

VERMICULITE and SHREDDED PEAT MOSS

5-10-5 FERTILIZER

MIX WELL

58

shredded peat moss. Add ¾ cups of ground limestone, ¼ cup of 20 percent superphosphate, and ½ cup of 5–10–5 fertilizer. Add a little water to reduce the amount of dust and mix thoroughly.

You can also buy a potting soil mixture, ready mixed and sterilized. Most commercial prepared mixtures, however, are too fine. Add 1 part coarse perlite to 3 parts soil. Mix thoroughly.

Topsoil in 50-pound bags is generally available at garden centers and can be used in container planting.

what to plant

Almost any kind of a flowering or foliage plant can be grown indoors. Growth depends upon the amount of soil and moisture in the air. Miniature vegetables are best for container planting.

Among the vegetable plants that will grow well are beets, carrots, herbs, garden cress, leaf lettuce, parsley, peppers, radishes, and dwarf tomatoes. (The Tiny Tim tomato thrives in a container.)

While you may hear suggestions for bigger plants, it seems to me that larger containers are awkward to work with.

light

60 Most vegetable plants grow better in full sunlight. Leafy and root vegetables can stand some shade.

planting

Read through Chapter 6.

You can start plants indoors by a month or so early and move them outside after the weather gets warmer.

To make a planting hole, use your finger or a pencil to the correct depth. Put in 2 or 3 seeds and cover with soil. Moisten.

fertilizer

Feeding is necessary for plants in containers, but do not overfertilize. Plant food comes in liquid, powder, and pellets. Read labels carefully and choose the fertilizer that is right for your plants and most convenient. Follow the directions carefully.

general care

You will need to use stakes on many of your plants. Follow the suggestions in Chapter 7.

chapter 12

extra fun in the garden

a playhouse

You can build a temporary playhouse with vines grown from gourd seeds. The vines are strong and leafy.

Gourds are the oddly shaped squash-like fruit used for decorations. A long time ago, farmers used the "dipper" gourd (after removing the seeds from the dry gourd) as a cup with which to dip water from the well.

63

here's what you need:

4 sturdy 5-foot wooden stakes (old broomsticks may be used)
nails and hammer
mesh chicken wire (or cord)
packet of small, mixed variety gourds

here's what you do:

1. Draw a square the size you want for your playhouse.
2. Measure the total distance of three sides for the amount of chicken wire you will need. (You can substitute rows of cord.)
3. Pound stakes into ground as deeply as you can at each corner of the square. (You may need adult help.)
4. Nail the chicken wire to the four poles. Leave one side as an opening. Make certain there are no rough edges. Cover with masking tape if necessary.
5. Following instructions on packet of gourds, dig a trench outside the wire and plant seeds.

64

6. As the vines grow, arrange them so that they climb up the wire and over. Leave the top open, however, to let in the sunshine.

a bean tent

You can make a summer-cool tent and grow vegetables at the same time.

here's what you need:
5 or 6 sturdy 6-foot poles
nails and hammer
wire (or cord)
packet of Kentucky Wonder Beans

here's what you do:
1. Place 5 or 6 poles in a wide circle leaning toward the top. Tie together at top with heavy cord or piece of wire (clothes hanger will do).
2. Starting at the bottom, circle the poles with wire or heavy cord all the way to the top. Remember to leave a space for the opening. Leave about 5 inches between rows. Hammer in nails to keep wire in place.
3. Following instructions on packet of beans, dig a trench around the base of the poles and plant beans.
4. As beans grow, arrange vines to climb upward on the wire or cord to the top. Beans grow very quickly.

65

a peanut patch

If you have enough space, and loose or sandy soil, you can grow your own peanuts. You need about 120 days from time of planting to maturity after the last frost. The directions on the packet are very clear.

Even if you don't have a lot of space, you might plant in a corner. Try a few in large, deep pots in the house near a very sunny window.

initials in a flower bed

You can make the initials of your school, such as ACS, or a design of your choice.

You need a piece of ground about 7 feet by 20 feet for initials, but a design can be done in a smaller area.

You may use seeds or plants.

Keep in mind that the background will be a solid mass of color in which the lines of the design in another color will stand out.

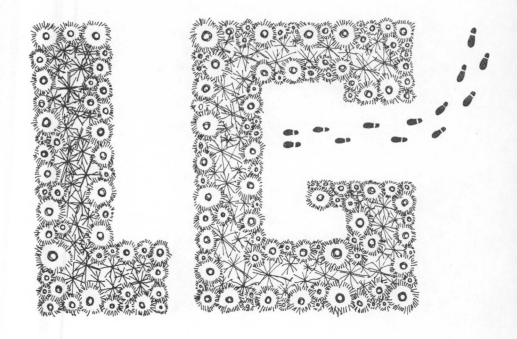

here's what you need:

1 packet of Ageratum Floss Flower, blue (small heads)
1 packet of Alyssum, white or pink
string and several stakes
tape measure or yardstick

here's what you do:

1. Draw design on paper with exact measurements. (Height of initials might be 5 feet, with width 1 foot.)
2. Decide use of colors. Lines might be white and background blue.
3. Mark off square or oblong of soil. Prepare according to instructions in Chapter 3.

4. Measure design on the ground and dig trenches according to plan.
5. Plant seeds or transplant plants, as directed in previous chapters.
6. When plants reach proper height, keep trimmed so that lines remain neat.

where to get more information

You can obtain excellent information from the county agricultural agents in your area. They are listed in the telephone directory under the county name and identified as Extension Service, Agriculture.

If you are in a large city which has a botanical garden, they too will give you information.

69

When you are in your local library, look at the gardening magazines. Many of the ads offer free printed material.

The federal government prints useful information. Write the Superintendent of Documents, Government Printing Office, Washington, D.C. 20250 for the following:

"List of Available Publications of the USDA," Bulletin ✕11, 45¢
"Minigardens for Vegetables," H & G Bulletin ✕163, 15¢
"Safe Use of Pesticides in the Home, in the Garden," PA ✕589

You can get these publications more quickly by writing your congressman, who usually sends one copy free to people in his or her district.

Seed catalogues can be gotten without cost from seed companies. Here are the names of some of the larger companies:

Burgess Seed and Plant Co.
P.O. Box 3000
Galesburg, Michigan 49053

W. Atlee Burpee Company
P.O. Box 6929
Philadelphia, Pennsylvania 19132

Henry Field Seed and Nursery Company
407 Sycamore Street
Shenandoah, Iowa 51602

Earl May Seed and Nursery Company
6032 Elm Street
Shenandoah, Iowa 51601

Here are the names of some of the smaller companies specializing in their regions:

Gurney Seed and Nursery
   Company
1448 Page Street   (northern)
Yankton, S. Dakota 57078

Joseph Harris Company, Inc.
Moreton Farm   (northeast)
Rochester, New York 14624

McFayden
P.O. Box 1600   (Canada and
Brandon, Manitoba,   northern USA)
   Canada

George W. Park Seed
   Company, Inc.
Greenwood, South Carolina   (southern)
   29646

Roswell Seed Company
P.O. Box 725   (southwest)
Roswell, New Mexico 88201

words you may not know

Bone meal: ground animal bone used for fertilizer. It dissolves slowly.

Clay soil: made up of very small particles which hold the water instead of allowing it to circulate.

Companion plants: those that influence each other for good or for bad.

Compost: a combination of vegetation and fertilizer that is allowed to decay. Used for fertilizing and rebuilding soil.

72

Fertilizer: a substance that enriches the soil. May be organic or inorganic.

Germination: sprouting of a plant from seed.

Humus: dark-brown substance resulting from decaying plant or animal residues, necessary for fertile soil.

Inorganic: not from plants or animals, from mineral or chemical substances.

Loam: soil containing a mixture of clay, sand, and humus.

Manure: livestock dung used as fertilizer, preferably decayed and dried out.

Mulch: a covering laid on soil between plants. Can be peat moss, compost, or grass clippings.

Nematode: a parasitic worm that cannot be seen by the eye. It infects plants and animals.

Nitrogen: an important plant nutrient.

Nutrient: any of the sixteen elements needed by plants.

Organic: anything from plants or animals; fertilizers of plant or animal origin.

Peat moss: humus resulting from sphagnum moss.

Perlite: crushed volcanic rock that helps absorb excess moisture in soil. Serves same purpose as sand.

Rotenone: insecticide made from a tropical shrub.

Sand: tiny particles of silicon and rocks which allow air and water to move through soil.

Seedling: a young plant.

Soil: upper level of earth in which plants may take root and grow. A combination of physical, chemical, and biological substances.

Succession planting: seeding a new crop as soon as or a little before the old one is harvested.

Thinning: pulling up seedlings to leave desired space between plants for growth.

Topsoil: the first layer of soil which has fine rock particles and decayed organic matter.

Vermiculite: artificial planting material made of mica. Used to increase water absorbency of soils. Serves as starting material indoors for seeds or plant cuttings.

Wood ash: burnt wood or charcoal ash.

index

75

Clay pots, 57
Clay soil, 24, 72
Clubs, garden, 8
Coffee can, use in fertilizing, 42
Coleus, 36
Commercial fertilizers, 20–21
Community gardening, 8
Companion planting, 47, 72
Compost (compost pile), 21–22,
    55, 72; "mini," 22
Container planting, 56–62;
    containers for, 57; fertilizer for,
    62; light for, 60; method of, 61;
    plants for, 59–60; soil for, 58–59
County Agricultural Agents, 8,
    17, 27, 31, 69
Cress: in containers, 59; garden
    (curly) or water, 14, 34, 59;
    planting guide, 34, 59
Crumbly soil, 23–24
Cucumbers, 14, 28; beetle
    control, 47; planting guide, 34
Cultivator, use of, 20, 42
Curly cress. See under Cress
Cutting back plants, 52
Cutworms, control of, 49

Dandelion (weed), 41
Definitions (words), gardening,
    72–74
Delphinium, cutting, 52
Designs, with flowers, 66–68
"Dipper" gourd, 63
Diseases. See Insect and disease
    control
Drainage: choosing garden site
    and, 14; container planting
    and, 57
Drying flowers, 52
Dwarf peas, 34
Dwarf tomatoes, 8, 59

Ecology, gardening and
    awareness of, 9–10

Eggplant, 29; staking, 45;
    transplanting, 39
Extension Service, Agriculture, 8,
    69; agents, 8 (see also County
    Agricultural Agents); soil
    testing and, 15

Federal government, as
    information source, 70
Fertilizers, 20–22, 24–25, 41–42,
    54–55, 72, 73; and care of
    garden, 41–42, 54–55;
    commercial, 20–21; compost
    pile, 21–22; for container plants,
    62; and getting garden ready
    for next year, 54–55; and
    preparing soil for planting,
    24–25, 54–55
5-10-5 fertilizer, 21, 25, 59
5-10-10 fertilizer, 21, 25
Flower bed, initials in, 66–68
Flowers, 27–29 (see also specific
    kinds); care of garden and
    (see Care of garden); choosing
    garden site for, 13, 14; drying,
    52; easy-to-grow, 28; how to
    plant, 37–38; initials (designs)
    from, 66–68; insect and disease
    control, 46–50; picking, 51–52;
    planting guide, 36, 37–38;
    preparing soil for, 23–26; size
    of garden for, 13; thinning,
    42–43; what to plant, 27–29;
    when to plant, 30–36
Four O'Clocks, 28; planting
    guide, 36
Frost date, when to plant and, 31
Fungicides. See Insecticides and
    fungicides

Garden clubs, 8
Garden cress. See under Cress
Gardening magazines, 69
Garden playhouse, making, 63–64

Seedlings: defined, 74; thinning, 42–43

Seeds (*see also* specific plants): buying, 28–29; care of garden and (*see* Care of garden); how to plant, 37–38; planting guide and tips, 34–36, 37–38; planting hole for, 37–38, 61; preparing ground for, 23–26; tape planting, 38; thinning seedlings, 42–43; watering, 44; what to plant, 30–37; when to plant, 30–36

Setting out (resetting) plants, 39

Sevin, 50

Shovel, use of, 19–25

Silt, 24

Size of garden, 13–14

Slugs, control of, 49

Snakes, for insect control, 48

Snap beans, 28 (*see also* Bush snap beans); harvesting, 52; planting guide, 34

Snapdragons, cutting, 52

Soil, 23–26, 74; care of garden and, 40–45 (*see also* Care of garden); choosing garden site and, 14–15; choosing what to grow and, 28; and container planting, 58–59; getting garden ready for next year and, 54–55; how to plant and, 37–38, 54–55; insect and pest control and, 46–50; kinds, what it is, 23–24, 73; planting guide and tips and, 34, 36, 37–38; preparing for planting, 23–26, 54–55; and setting out plants, 39; substitutes, 58–59; testing, 15, 23; texture of, 23, 24

Spacing: thinning and, 42; vegetables, 34–35

Spade (spading), 19, 25, 55; and turning garden over, 55

Spinach, transplanting, 43

Sprays and powders, chemical. *See* Insecticides and fungicides

Squash, 28, 35; bugs, control of, 47; harvesting, 53; planting guide, 35; summer, 35, 53

Stakes, metal or wooden, use of, 19, 24, 37, 38; container planting and, 62; for garden playhouse, 64; staking method, 45; in transplanting, 39

Stock (flower), 36

Strawflower: drying, 52; planting guide, 36

String, to mark rows, 19, 24, 37

Succession planting, 32, 74

Summer squash. *See under* Squash

Sunflower, 28; planting guide, 36

Sunshine (sunlight): choosing garden site for, 14; indoor planting and, 60; planting guide, 34–36 (*see also* specific flowers, vegetables); transplanting, 39

Superphosphate, use of, 59. *See also* Phosphate fertilizer

Tapes, seed, 38

Tent, bean, making, 65

Testing of soil, 15, 23

Thinning plants, 42–43, 74

Tides, planting by the moon cycle and, 33

Tidiness, care of garden and, 43, 54; with tools, 20

Time, how much to spend on gardening, 15

Times for planting (when to plant), 31–36; flower guide, 36; moon cycle and, 32–33; succession planting and, 32;